Amazing Nature

Incredible Life Cycles

D1091844

Tim Knight

Heinemann Library
Chicago, Illinois

Printed and bound in the Hong Kong, China by South China Printing

07 06 05 04 03
10 9 8 7 6 5 4 3 2 1

Library of Congress Cataloging-in-Publication Data

  Incredible life cycles / Tim Knight.
      p. cm. -- (Amazing nature)
Summary: Explains the circle of life in the plant and animal kingdoms, from reproduction, through their growing years as they adapt to their habitats, to their deaths.
Includes bibliographical references and index.
  ISBN 1-4034-1148-4 (lib. bdg.-hardcover) -- ISBN 1-4034-3258-9 (pbk.)
  1. Life cycles (Biology)--Juvenile literature. [1. Life cycles (Biology)] I. Title.
  QH501.K56 2003
  571.8--dc21
                        2002153989

Acknowledgments
The publisher would like to thank the following for permission to reproduce photographs:
pp. 4, 11 Stephen Dalton/NHPA; pp. 5, 17 Gerard Lacz/FLPA; p. 6 Jurgen Freund/Nature Picture Library; p. 7 Michael & Patricia Fogden/Corbis; pp. 8, 21 B. Jones & M. Shimlock/NHPA; p. 9 John Hawkins; p. 10 A.N.T./NHPA; pp. 12 (left), 16 (top) Minden Pictures/FLPA; pp. 12 (right) Masahiro Lijima/Ardea; p. 13 Rudie Kuiter/OSF; p. 14 Chris Knights/Ardea; p. 15 John Watkins/FLPA; p. 16 (bottom) Brake/Sunset/FLPA; pp. 18, 25 (right) Tim Knight; pp. 19, 24 Ron Austing/FLPA; pp. 20, 25 (left) Anthony Bannister/NHPA; p. 22 Martin Harvey/NHPA; p. 23 Terry Whittaker/FLPA; p. 26 Kim Taylor/Bruce Coleman; p. 27 Jean-Paul Ferrero/Ardea

Cover photo: Stephen Dalton/NHPA

Some words are shown in bold, **like this.** You can find out what they mean by looking in the glossary.

Contents

Circle of Life

A giant rain forest tree that towers 330 feet (70 meters) above the forest floor, started life as a tiny seed. The tree has to survive many events to reach this age and size. For example, it has to avoid being eaten when it is a tiny **sapling.** It also has to fight for its share of sunlight as it grows taller. And it has to be strong enough not to be blown down by a violent storm. Someday, however, it will crash to the ground, rot, and disappear forever. During its life the tree will have made millions of seeds. Some of those seeds may grow to be as big as the parent tree.

This is an example of the millions of life cycles that are going on around us every day. As you read this book, seeds everywhere are turning into plants. A baby crocodile is hatching from its egg. A blue whale calf is leaving its mother's side. A snake is shedding its skin. An ancient rain forest tree is falling to the ground.

This book deals with each stage of life, from birth through death. It takes a close look at the weird and wonderful lives of animals, plants, and other **organisms,** and at some of the mind-boggling changes they go through.

A bracken fern protects its young leaves by filling them with cyanide poison.

By the time a baby chimpanzee is fully grown, it will have learned how to find and eat hundreds of different types of food and to **communicate** in over 30 different ways. It may even be able to use simple tools.

Mass Production

Animals produce their young in different ways. Most **mammals** give birth to live young. Birds and many snakes and lizards lay eggs. Not all animals take care of their young. Many parents leave their **offspring** alone in a world full of hungry **predators**. If an animal or plant produces as many eggs or seeds as possible, there is a chance that at least one or two of its offspring may survive. That is enough for a new **generation**.

On Christmas Island in the Indian Ocean, up to 100 million land crabs scuttle down to the seashore. They go there so they can **spawn** at exactly the same time. Each female produces about 100,000 eggs. By the time all the females have finished spawning, the water looks like a thick soup. Mass spawning is especially common among sea creatures such as jellyfish, shellfish, and coral.

Every year swarms of red land crabs leave their forest burrows on Christmas Island and head down to the sea to lay eggs.

Blowing in the wind

For a flowering plant to **reproduce,** its **pollen** must reach another flower of the same kind. Grasses and many trees depend on the wind to carry their pollen. These plants produce billions of grains of pollen. With a bit of luck, a few grains will be blown in the right direction and reach the right flower.

Puffballs and other mushrooms produce **spores.** These miniature specks of life are carried off on the breeze.

Survival of the Luckiest

An animal or plant that depends on **mass production** has no control over what happens to its eggs or seeds. A Christmas Island crab can do nothing to keep its eggs or the babies that hatch from being eaten by fish. When a plant scatters its seeds, there is a chance that none of the seeds will survive.

Most turtles nest on a quiet, sandy beach. The female turtle uses her flippers to dig a hole above the high-tide mark. After laying her eggs, she covers them with sand. Once they hatch, baby turtles must reach the sea without being eaten. If the turtle **hatchlings** were to cross the sand one at a time, they would each end up as a bite-sized snack for a hungry **predator.** Instead, all the eggs hatch at about the same time. With so many baby turtles racing down the beach at once, there is too much food even for the greedy gulls and lizards that gather for the feast. Some lucky hatchlings make it safely to the sea.

These newly hatched green turtles will use their tiny flippers to drag themselves down to the ocean.

When a jay buries an acorn, it sometimes marks the spot with a small stone.

Acorns to oaks

Some plants depend on animals to spread their seeds around. A fully grown oak tree makes thousands of acorns every fall. Deer may eat those that fall to the ground, leaving them somewhere else in their droppings. Squirrels and birds, such as jays, pluck them straight from the tree and store them for later. Jays bury their acorns carefully to hide them from other animals. But they cannot remember every single hiding place. Safely planted in the soil, the few forgotten acorns **germinate** and grow into oak trees.

Special Care

Animals that take care of their **offspring** have many unusual ways of caring for them.

Emperor penguins live in Antarctica. The female lays just one large egg. She lifts it quickly onto her feet before it freezes on the ice. Her mate then rolls it onto his own feet. He warms it under a special fold of skin that is covered in feathers. The male **incubates** the egg while the female walks about 90 miles (150 kilometers) across the ice to find food in the sea. He stands in the freezing cold until the female returns 60 days later, just in time to feed the newly hatched chick.

Emperor penguin chicks hitch a ride on their fathers' feet to avoid standing on the freezing ice.

The female Surinam toad uses her own body as a nest. Before she **spawns,** she grows a thick spongy pad on her back. After the male has pressed the **fertilized** eggs into this sticky sponge, a skin grows over them. Now they are safe from **predators**. Three months later, the eggs will have grown into tiny toads. They break the skin and climb out of the holes in their mother's back.

Wasp food

Even those animals that do not care for their young sometimes help them by leaving behind a supply of food. One giant **parasitic** wasp feeds its **larvae** bird-eating spiders. The wasp stings the spider so that it cannot move. She bites off its legs and carries the body back to her nest. Here she lays an egg on the still-living spider and buries it. When the wasp larva hatches, it eats the spider alive.

Scorpions give birth to living babies. The newborn scorpions climb onto their mother's back and stay with her until they are old enough to look after themselves.

Switching Jobs

Male emperor penguins may seem like superdads. But some other fathers in the animal kingdom work just as hard to help their **offspring.**

The rhea looks like a small scruffy ostrich. The male rhea makes a nest by scraping a hole in the ground. He **mates** with several females. Each female lays her eggs in his nest. In the end, there may be 50 or more eggs in the pile. The male **incubates** them all by himself. When the eggs hatch, he raises the young rheas.

Bird Links

The African ostrich, the South American rhea, and the Australian emu are all long-legged birds that cannot fly. Although they live on different continents, they look and act alike. All three birds eat grass and live on the open plains.

A male emu keeps an eye on his newly hatched chicks.

The eggs in this nest belong to many different females. The young will hatch after about 45 days.

Pregnant dads

The male seahorse actually gives birth! Male seahorses have pouches on their bellies. A female lays hundreds of eggs in a male's pouch. Her job is now over. The male seals the eggs inside his pouch and carries them around. He feeds the growing eggs with a fluid produced by the pouch. A male seahorse can give birth to more than 1,000 babies in 24 hours.

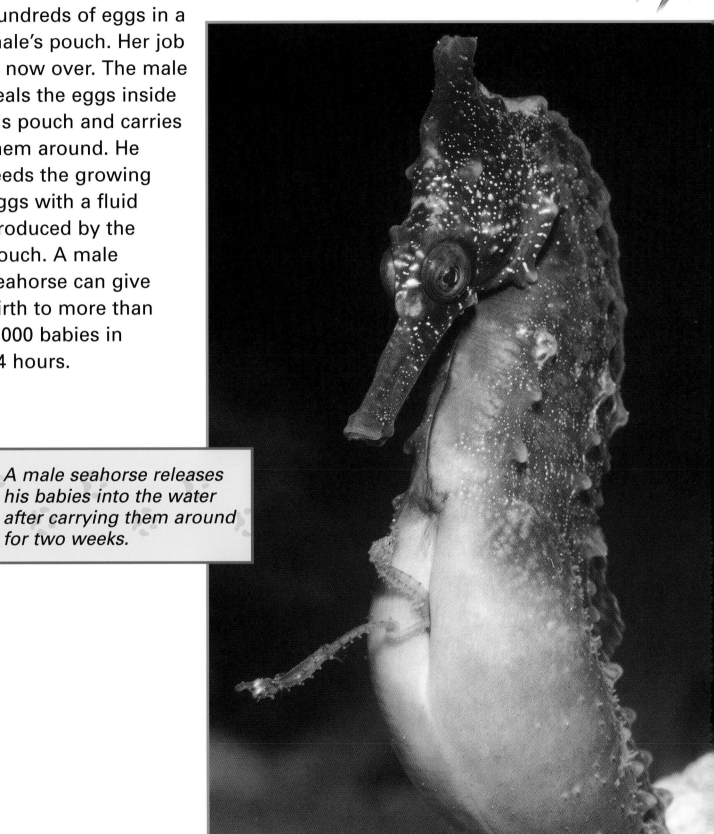

A male seahorse releases his babies into the water after carrying them around for two weeks.

Help Yourself

Some animals must take care of themselves as soon as they are born. They have to watch for enemies right away. The **venom** of a newly hatched king cobra is just as poisonous as that of an adult snake. There are a lot of hungry hunters on the African plains. A young gnu or zebra can run within five minutes of being born.

A newborn zebra trots after its mother. Zebras carry their young for twelve months before giving birth.

A newly hatched cuckoo's first act is to throw out the offspring of its foster parents.

Nursery crime

Cuckoos save themselves the trouble of raising a family by laying their eggs in other birds' nests. Birds that do this are called brood parasites. The unlucky foster parents are known as hosts. When the young cuckoo hatches, it pushes any other eggs or **offspring** out of the nest. This means that the cuckoo chick gets all the food and all the attention of its new parents.

Nursery climb

A newborn kangaroo's first trip is the shortest it will ever make but probably the hardest. It has to climb a distance of about 8 inches (20 centimeters) to reach one of the nipples in its mother's pouch. The tiny pink baby cannot see or hear, so it takes it about three minutes to make the journey. It drags itself upward through its mother's fur with the help of miniature claws. Once it has found a nipple, it remains attached for a whole month. Without its mother's milk, it would quickly die.

Early Learning Center

Some parents stay around to help their **offspring** through the first dangerous days of life. Others stay with their young for months or years. They teach them how to survive and pass on what they know. The more there is to learn, the longer the lessons last.

Lion cubs need to practice their hunting skills.

When baby crocodiles are about to hatch, they squeak loudly. The mother digs down to her eggs and helps them out. She carefully picks up the babies in her jaws. She then carries them to a quiet stretch of the riverbank. The baby crocodiles stay in their riverbank home for two months. They are closely guarded by their parents all this time.

A crocodile moves its newly hatched young to safety.

Helping out

Raising a family is hard work. Some parents help each other by looking after large numbers of youngsters while the other parents rest or look for food. Ostriches, eider ducks, and cavies (related to the guinea pig) are just a few of the animals that leave their children in a nursery.

Elephants live in **extended families** led by an older female, known as the matriarch. Most of the other adults are her sisters, daughters, and granddaughters. When a baby elephant is born, the whole herd gets involved. All the adults look after the calf as it grows.

Some baby elephants may be ten years old before they leave their mother's side.

Crowded House

Bees, wasps, ants, and termites all live in big **colonies.** A termite mound is home to more than a million tiny insects. They all belong to one family. The family is made up of workers and soldiers. The workers build and fix the family home, gather food, and clean. Soldier termites stand guard, defending the colony with their large jaws.

The queen is huge. She is almost 5 inches (12 centimeters) long and too fat to move. She is really nothing more than an egg-laying machine. She lays about 30,000 each day. The colony has only one male, the king, that can **mate** with the queen.

The members of the colony **communicate** using special chemicals that pass between them whenever they touch.

The walls of a termite mound are built from a mixture of earth and saliva that gets as hard as concrete.

Naked mole-rats spend their whole lives underground. They eat plant roots and bulbs.

Naked mole-rats also live in large underground colonies. They have pink skin and no fur. They are almost blind. They use their sharp front teeth to dig tunnels as they search for fat, juicy plant roots. Their underground home is divided into sleeping quarters, nurseries, and food storage areas.

The naked mole-rats are different sizes and do different jobs. The smallest are the workers. They do all the digging. A few of the young workers grow bigger than the rest. They move back into the nest area where they help feed the babies. The mole-rats that grow biggest of all become soldiers. They spend most of their time sleeping. They need to save their energy for when the colony is in danger. If a snake sneaks into one of the rooms, the soldiers will attack it. Their teeth are powerful enough to kill most unwanted visitors.

Growing Up

Some animals and plants grow very quickly. Bamboo plants grow as much as 3 feet (1 meter) per day. That's almost fast enough for us to see it happening with our own eyes. The deep-sea clam is one of the slowest-growing creatures. It takes it up to 100 years to reach one-third of an inch (8 millimeters). On the other hand, a blue whale calf doubles its length to about 43 feet (13 meters) and triples its weight to nearly 20,000 pounds (9,000 kilograms) in just six months.

Some animals outgrow their skin. A caterpillar is basically a stomach on legs. When its skin gets too small for it, the caterpillar **molts**. A new skin has grown underneath. A **sloughing** snake peels off its skin in much the same way, scraping away the old scales by crawling over a rough surface.

The colorful tiger snake is even more dazzling when it has just shed its skin.

As it grows, a hermit crab protects itself with a series of tightly fitting shell suits.

Shell houses

Crabs, lobsters, and other **crustaceans** are protected by a hard shell. They can only grow by shedding it. When a crab is ready to molt, it grows a new skin under its shell. The old shell splits and the crab steps out. A crab has no protection against enemies until its new shell hardens. Hermit crabs avoid this problem by making their home inside the empty shell of some other creature. When they have outgrown their house, they simply move into a bigger shell.

Changes

All plants and animals change as they grow. Some simply keep growing bigger. Others may change shape or color. Male lions usually grow a shaggy mane. As a deer grows up, it loses the spotted coat that helped it blend in with its surroundings. Birds quickly lose their egg tooth, the hard point on their beak that helped them break out of their shell when they first hatched.

A baby elephant seal triples its weight during the first three weeks of its life. Drinking its mother's extra-rich milk, the baby seal grows into a 330-pound (150-kilogram) pile of blubber. At this stage, it is left to take care of itself. It begins to lose weight again as its body grows stronger. Over the next two months, it sheds its coat of warm fur and changes shape from a fat blob to a **streamlined** swimmer.

A lion's thick, woolly mane warns others that he is strong and powerful.

Complete change

Other creatures change so much that the new body looks nothing like the old body it replaced. Scientists call this **metamorphosis.** The most amazing example of this is the life cycle of a butterfly. Caterpillars spend their lives feeding, growing, and **molting.** When they have reached full size, they turn into a **pupa** that is wrapped in a hard, protective covering called a chrysalis. Inside the chrysalis an incredible change is taking place. When a dazzling butterfly breaks free of its chrysalis, it is hard to believe that it was once a fat caterpillar.

For the first few weeks of its life, a baby tapir has a striped and spotted coat. This pattern breaks up its outline and helps it hide.

Hidden Lives

Some plant and animal life cycles are almost totally secret. We only discover what happens when they put in a sudden, usually short, appearance.

During the first few years of its life, an insect called a cicada is never seen. The wingless **larva** spends up to seventeen years underground, where it eats plant roots. Then, the fully grown larva tunnels up to the surface. It crawls out through a chimney of soil and climbs up the nearest plant stem. Minutes later, the larva's skin splits open and an adult cicada climbs out.

After an adult cicada leaves its old skin, it takes it a few minutes to pump up its wings.

Wasp and fig

The strangler fig needs the help of a tiny wasp to live. The wasp spends most of its life hidden within a fig fruit. A fig tree's flowers are inside its fruit. Female fig wasps enter through a hole in the ripe fruit. They carry **pollen** from the male flowers in the fig fruit where they were born. As they lay their eggs inside the new fig, they leave pollen in its female flowers. Fig wasp larvae then grow inside the fig. The males hatch first and find a female and **mate** with her. The males, which have no eyes or wings, then die without ever having left the fig. The winged females push their way out and fly to another fig, picking up pollen as they leave.

A tiny black fig wasp can be seen among the flowers of this ripe fig.

*Fungi have no stems, roots, or leaves. Most of the time, their body is a network of connected threads, hidden in soil or rotting wood. When mushrooms suddenly pop up overnight, they seem to have come from nowhere. After shedding their **spores,** they disappear again without a trace.*

Old Age

It can take a plant or animal as little as a few days to as much as thousands of years to complete its life cycle.

Bristlecone pine trees grow in the southwestern United States. They are thought to live longer than any other plant in the world. The oldest bristlecone pine is more than 4,700 years old. Animals have shorter life cycles. The giant tortoises of the Galapagos Islands are the oldest living animals. They may live for 175 years or more.

Australia's Great Barrier Reef is built from millions of tiny coral animals. Each is just a few millimeters across. The lifetime of a single coral is short. But the whole reef has been alive for 500 million years.

*Many adult mayflies live for only 24 hours—just long enough to find a **mate**.*

A fallen tree trunk takes many years to rot. Fungi, beetles, and termites eat away at it until it completely disappears.

New from old

The death of a giant rain forest tree offers life to a new **generation** of plants, including its own seeds. When it falls, it may knock down other trees in its path, leaving a huge gap in the forest. Suddenly sunlight can reach the forest floor, finally giving the tiny plants there enough energy for a life of their own. It is the signal for another of nature's life cycles to begin again.

Fact File

The honey fungus may be the largest living **organism.** Scientists discovered that underground threads covering an area of 2,200 acres were all connected to the same individual. The fungus is 2,400 years old.

The world's biggest **mollusk,** the giant clam, spurts out 500 million eggs at a time. This clam may **spawn** 40 years in a row.

A newborn panda is smaller than a mouse and weighs about 3.5 ounces (100 grams).

The tenrec of Madagascar, a kind of giant shrew, holds the record for the largest number of **offspring** produced by a mammal. One tenrec gave birth to 32 babies.

A newborn giraffe is 6 feet (1.8 meters) tall and doubles its height in its first year.

The world's only egg-laying **mammals,** known as monotremes, are the platypus and the echidna.

A young kangaroo, known as a joey, does not leave its mother's pouch until it is at least seven months old.

The giant puffball fungus can grow as large as a soccer ball. It produces about 7.5 million **spores.** If every one of its spores grew into another puffball, they would weigh as much as 20,000 elephants.

An opossum is pregnant for only thirteen days before giving birth.

One type of North American mouse has up to seventeen **litters** of babies in a single breeding season for a total of 150 young.

Ostrich eggs are the largest in the world. They can measure 4.3 inches (11 centimeters) by 7 inches (18 centimeters) and weigh 3.3 pounds (1.5 kilograms).

Originally about 490 feet (150 meters) tall, the eucalyptus tree at Watts River, Victoria, Australia is the tallest tree ever.

The coco de mer, a palm tree found only in the Seychelles, has nuts weighing about 44 pounds (20 kilograms).

The blue whale, the largest animal on the planet, can be nearly 100 feet (30 meters) long and weigh more than 25 elephants.

A queen bee can lay up to 2,000 eggs in a single day.

One kind of cichlid fish protects its eggs by sucking them into its own mouth. Once the babies hatch, they stay in their parent's mouth until they are a week old.

Glossary

colony large group of the same kind of animal

communicate share information

crustacean creature, such as a crab, protected by a hard or soft shell

extended family family group that includes aunts, uncles, cousins, and grandparents

fertilized when male and female sex cells have been brought together in order to produce young

generation group of plants or animals that came into being during the same time period

germinate begin to grow

hatchling animal that has just hatched from an egg

incubate warm (eggs) by sitting on them

larva/larvae stage in the life of an insect. A larva hatches from an egg and looks like a little worm.

litter group of newborn animals

mammal animal that feeds on its mother's milk

mass production making something, such as eggs or seeds, in very large amounts

mate partner. Also, what a male and female animal do to start an egg or baby growing inside the female.

metamorphosis process that changes a young animal into a very different looking adult

mollusk sea animal that has a shell covering its body

molt shed feathers, hair, or skin

offspring babies or young animals

organism living animal or plant

parasitic feeding on another living animal or plant

pollen sticky powder made by flowers

predator animal that hunts and kills other living creatures for food

pupa stage in an insect's life that follows the larva stage. During the pupa stage, the insect develops into a winged adult.

reproduce produce young

sapling young tree

slough shed old skin

spawn lay groups of eggs in the water

spore seed-like speck produced by fungi to help them reproduce

streamlined smooth and pointed to improve movement through air or water

venom poison made inside the bodies of certain animals, such as snakes, spiders, and lizards

Further Reading

Fleisher, Paul. *Life Cycles of a Dozen Diverse Creatures.* Brookfield, Conn.: Millbrook Press, 1998.

Riha, Susanne. *Animal Journeys: Life Cycles and Migrations.* San Diego: Blackbirch Press, 1999.

Stalio, Ivan. *Life Cycles.* Austin, Texas: Raintree/Steck-Vaughn, 1998.

Index